# Death of a Statue

*Poems*

## Samuel Chuma

Mwanaka Media and Publishing Pvt Ltd,
Chitungwiza Zimbabwe
*
*Creativity, Wisdom and Beauty*

Publisher: *Mmap*

Mwanaka Media and Publishing Pvt Ltd
24 Svosve Road, Zengeza 1
Chitungwiza Zimbabwe
mwanaka@yahoo.com
mwanaka13@gmail.com
https://www.mmapublishing.org
www.africanbookscollective.com/publishers/mwanaka-media-and-publishing
https://facebook.com/MwanakaMediaAndPublishing/

Distributed in and outside N. America by African Books Collective
orders@africanbookscollective.com
www.africanbookscollective.com

ISBN: 978-1-77931-488-8
EAN: 9781779314888

© Samuel Chuma 2023

**DISCLAIMER**
All views expressed in this publication are those of the author and do not necessarily reflect the views of *Mmap*.

# DEDICATION

This book is dedicated to the memory of my late mother, *Sarah Chuma* and to the memory of my late father, *Ben Mashingaidze* and to the memory of my late aunt *Jessica Makadzinga Baye* nee *Mashingaidze*

# TABLE OF CONTENTS

# Foreword

"Death of a Statue" is a collection of poems that explore spiritual, religious, social, moral, and interpersonal themes. Each poem delves into the complexities of the human experience, examining the joys and sorrows that we all encounter at different points in our lives. From love and loss to faith and doubt, these poems offer a glimpse into the myriad emotions and struggles that define our existence.

The title of this anthology, "Death of a Statue," is both symbolic and literal. On one level, it refers to the destruction of physical statues, which have become a controversial topic in recent years. On a deeper level, it speaks to the idea that our ideals and beliefs can crumble and fall, leaving us with a sense of loss and uncertainty. The poems in this collection grapple with these themes, exploring the ways in which we find meaning and purpose in a world that can often feel chaotic and uncertain.

At their core, these poems are a celebration of the human spirit. They remind us that even in our darkest moments, we have the capacity to find hope and meaning. They challenge us to confront our fears and doubts, and to embrace the full range of emotions that make us who we are. Whether you are searching for solace in times of grief, or simply looking for a deeper understanding of the human experience, "Death of a Statue" offers a powerful and inspiring journey through the joys and challenges of life.

As the editor of this anthology, I am honored to present these poems to you. Each one has been carefully selected for its insight, beauty, and emotional resonance. I hope that you will find in them a source of comfort, inspiration, and reflection, and that they will touch your heart in the way that they have touched mine

# MUKWERERA

it came without warning
and without welcome
like a priestly fart
during holy communion

it landed without ceremony
right in the froth of the sorghum brew
that the elders had ordered brewed
to quench the thirst of the spirits

So that perchance when full-bladdered
they would point their members earthwards
and shoot off celestial piss
into dry mouthed fields and vleis

it paddled and took a bath
right in grandpa's mug
he glared back at it
and took a mighty swallow

And spit it out
And as his saliva
hit the dust
it rained ......

## REFUGEES

Last night I looked at the sky
And beheld its vivid anger
As it roared with thunderous voice

Scaring virgin droplets
Of waters pure and innocent
And causing them to
Flee the heavens
For the dusty embrace
Of a gleeful earth
Which offered not
Its hand to afford
The refugees a soft landing

But only opens its mouth
To feed the insatiable
Rivers and lakes
That form its innards

# DELILAH

## 1
She loves hotly
As though she got
Embers coursing
In her veins
Fanning the furnaces
Of her hard as bricks,
Heart.

She got no chimney
Inbuilt to channel
The smoke of her passions

She got no extractor
To suck in fresh emotions
When her red-hot rage
Reduces her loving
To blackened cinders
That smolder endlessly
And peep out of her eyes
Mesmerizingly like
Python gait

## 2
I have heard mention
Of the river between
But none took the
Heart and time
To school me
How to navigate triumphantly
The treacherous
descent

Past thigh-like
mountains
Whose paths are
Not mapped on
Google earth
As I seek
The heaven fabled
To exist between
Her wantonness
And my need

# BIRDSONG

How I wish I could
Like a bird speak
In a manner so coded
That when my mouth I open
The world would think
It's music

How funny it must be
To the robin in forest glade
That when it opens its mouth
To utter bird tales
To its kith and kindred
Uncultured men eavesdrop
And at once
Outdo each the other
To pen sonnets teary
And hypnotic
To beguile a humanity
Whose language is
Of make up coarse,

Such that when birds talk
They dance to the tune.

# MESSIAH

The river died
Right before my eyes
It gave up the spook
One moment like a lion
It was roaring with swagger
The next it was
For breath struggling
Valiantly putting up
A show of being alright
Yet it was dying

I saw fish and frogs
Desert it in droves
As if they by disassociation
Would gain immortality
They did not even tarry
To pay their last respects
To the comrade who
In weather fair and foul
Stood by them

Only the sky wept
Fat torrential tears
And howled in
Thunderous anguish
And as its tears
Found space and accommodation
On the now dusty corpse
I saw as if in a dream
The river shake itself
Like Lazarus from

The tomb arisen
And with a mighty roar
Its bounds it unshackled
And sped with mighty
And triumphant glee
In pursuit of the water creatures
Who forsook it in
Its moments of demise

# SHADOWS

How do shadows feel
When light's uninvited hand
Pulls them from darkness' embrace
To display them in grotesque form
In a world oblivious
To their presence and welfare

How do they feel
When they are trampled upon
And dragged through
Fire and mud
And rendered unwilling companions
On journeys not of their interest
And being made to mimic
Actions tiring and maddening
Without consent or consultation

They too have
Families to care for
Left orphaned in dark abodes
Where light's intrusive forays
Are not received with joy
But are met with fear
And tremulous regard

# JEZEBEL

## 1

She looked at me
With innocent eyes
Like a doe beholding
The mesmerizing sight
Of mating pythons
Who for once for her
Pose no risk
As their hunger
Each for the other
Dwarfs the duty
To seek satisfaction
In stuffing the stomach.

## 2

She screamed like
A demon on fire
One hot day
When like a python
She wrapped her
Pliant limbs about
My hungry torso
As she shot me
To starry realms
Unbeknownst prior
Till down I came crashing
Into the pleasant prison
Of her doe eyes...

# THE DAY SHE LEFT

The day she left me
Was as barren as
A toddler's womb
No rains fell from
The heavens
No breeze blew
No sun, no blue sky
Just angry black clouds
And thick sulking heat

The day she left me
I tried to weep
But the tears fled
Locking themselves up
Within the tents of my pain
Cowering from the livid
Face of the day

The day she left me
Even my voice
Slunk backwards
Into my stomach
Like a cough in reverse
Seeking to escape
Aboard half digested
Pledges and vows

# AND THE BEES WEPT

The day died young
It died at dawn
Before its chubby fingers
Could disrobe and render naked
Fresh born flowers
Of the dewy apparel
They adorn to entice
Early morning bees
To drink and dilute
Their venom of its sting

It died in the arms
Of ancient mountains
Who howled with volcanic distress
And as their lava tears
Rolled down their granite cheeks
They raced down to the meadows
And razed down to nothingness
The flowers in their immobile grandeur

## SPACES

The pause in between
the naked sobs
of heartbroken widow

The empty growl
of hungry stomach
demanding sustenance

The near death
vacuumed gasp of
orgasmic release

The ruins of thought
Now colonized by
Ghosts of reason

The foundations of grief
Built upon naivety
And untamed expectations

The abode of pain
Where doors are unlocked
But joy remains captive

These are the spaces
That always find me
Lying prone and stupefied

And always they lead me
To pastures green
And at leisure rape me

# GAP-TOOTH

I wish i could
In size reduce
To dwarfish stature
And in that miniscule guise
Steal ever so stealthily
Past the sweet twinned
Hills of your lips
Where sweetness lies buried
To be excavated by the
Pneumatic drills of
Twisting tongues

And i would the magic words
That unlock the doors
Of your smile utter
And enter your mouth
Where teeth radiantly
Fashioned cohabit
In forced uniformity

And fit myself
Into that gap between
Your frontline teeth
And be part of the magic
That changes the universe
When you smile

## DEVIL SEED

When devils
With angels mate
The offspring is
A conflicting bundle
Of confusion
Reminiscent of that
Definitive day
When laid down
On church bench
You screamed out
To the heavens
As he rammed
Into your secret places
While the angels
Etched on church ceiling
Winked conspiratorially
As the devil seed in him
Burst out triumphantly
And spilled over
To the floor
Like the oil dripping
Off the beard of Aaron

## ROTTEN DAY

I wish today
was yesterday
When Dawn
Remembered
To brush her teeth
And scent her body
Before embracing
And kissing me
Good Morning

Today's unkempt morning
Planted its unhygienic lips
On my unguarded mouth
In a hopeless attempt
To wish me Good Day
Despite the discouraging stares
Of the livid infant sun

Thus awakening me from my slumber.
With the fetid smell
Of yesterday's dream-cadavers
And the musky fragrance
Of raped hopes
And aborted plans
Reeking with the odour
Of congealed menstrual flows
Eerily battling to stain
Today's underpants

## EXORCISM

Things feel so different
The vexed being
Remains at pain
To distinguish between
The alpha and the omega
And so stands still
Rooted in own indecision

The medicine man
Too is perplexed
The bones point
To a past peopled
By wraiths from the future
Humming Christian hymns
Inscribed on pagan tombstones

Will the priest
Fervently reciting the rosary
Manage to subdue
Powers of old falsely
Imprisoned as demonic entities
From rising to claim
Once and forevermore
Control of their bloodlines
In these times of hardship?

# AND THE TREES WEPT...

I'm free
I'm free
Sang the leaf
As it explored
Lofty heights
While gripped
In the loose embrace
Of a whirlwind
That had wrenched it
From the stoic embrace
Of its parent branch

I can soar higher than you
Screamed the ecstatic leaf
As it shot past
Dumbfounded eagles
Flying without wings
In the arms of a whirlwind
Whose strength was
Progressively waning

I can touch the heavens
Gushed the now euphoric leaf
And the whirlwind gave a groan
And unclasped its fingers
And down the screaming
Leaf came
Past bemused eagles
Lofted high above
The burning sands
Of the Sahara

## WORLD WIDE WEB

it is a scary place to be
where decency is discovered
half-chewed and cowered
in garbage bins
somewhere in the
back alleys of
a street named NOW

where manners
run for dear life
hotly pursued by
nimble-minded children
whose eyes are
constantly glued on
phone screens that
package and broadcast
vulgarity and lewdness
as humour and wit

and the priest
at his station
retrieves his own device
from the forest of
rosaries, incense
and holy writ
to ogle at nuns sitting
open-legged and available
in tik tok posts

## LOVE STORY

When love was
A beautiful place
To go
We would pay her
Frequent visits
And oft times we found
Her seated in her veranda
Humming age old hymns
And endlessly knitting
Mountains of babywear
With multi-coloured yarn

Other times, she would
Just sit there
With a faraway look
And we would hold
Our peace whilst
She took out
An ancient diary,

To recite for us
Poetry written in
Cherubim script
With starlight ink
That defied eons
And still sparkled
As it did when
The universe was
An infant still
To find its feet,

But one day
We found the veranda
Bereft of her aura
And all that remained

Was a pile of babywear
All of black color
Lying discarded with
The knitting needles
Supine silent and hungry
Without anyone to
Feed them yarn

Thus, we turned
Our backs on
Love's abode
And she went her way
And I mine
On that cruel day
When no knitting
Needles clicked...

# AN ODE FOR ELVIS

Death wears many faces
Mostly smiley ones
That rarely sneer

It wears many coats
Even merry-colored ones
Very like Joseph
But without the dream

Yesterday it wore
His brother's face
Hastily smeared on
Like a harlot's makeup

As it gorged itself
On tyre and gasoline
Belching smoke and fire
Like a dragon on the prowl

And like a dragon
It swooped on him suddenly
Burning him to cinder

And the last his
Anguished eyes saw
Was his brother's face
Smirking in triumph.

# OF DOGS, CATS AND MICE

It rained cats and dogs
And the mice cast fearful eyes
At the heavens
As they beheld mayhem
Come their way without invitation

This land has become
A habitation of hounds
Of hell and cat-faced angels
He said to no one in particular
One difficult day
When catfights were
The never changing
Background on celestial
Phone screens

Irked thunder roared
Ripped the sky open
Exposing incensed shooting stars
At target practice
Popping shots at the
Fleeing furry combatants

The mice are better
Protected in this war
Though some of them
Fall prey to stray malice
He continued sagely
And whereupon he wheezed
Coughed and spat blood
And said,

The day the mice
Are free of the war
Is the day that peace

Will shed off its coat
To adorn a dog's teeth
And a cat's paws
And go knocking on
Every mousey aboard
Claiming to have liberated
The mice from a war
That never was theirs.

## LOVE QUEST

He ransacked her closet
In a quest for love
But found instead
Blood-stained underwear
Cowering and shivering
In a shelf which housed
Unused condoms
And weeping hearts
And torn hymens...

He prayed for
healing rain
And the heavens
burst open
Somewhere deep
Inside his being
Birthing rivulets
That moved like
Lazy serpents on
His cheek-terrain
Headed nowhere
But to their doom.

## PLAYER

A while ago
Maybe six sad moons past
He sat on the hill of aspirations
Pregnant with the silent
power of an eagle
Grooming its talons
Before taking off
For a scheduled date
With a frail breasted dove.

He saw her appear
As if in a sensual dream
Holding in her hands
A heart dangerously
Innocent and pure
Each smiling step
Bringing her yet closer
To the bloodied altar
Of an age-old deity
Whose appetite for plunder
Knows no restraint.

She came accompanying
The sun at sunrise
Clothed with suicidal courage
Like the morning dew
Which flinches not
At the sun's fiery caress
But sparkles and dazzles
Albeit for a short while
Before expiring unceremoniously
In a misty haze

# THE RED SEA

She went to bed a child
Her arms wrapped around
Her sexless teddy bear
In easy alliance

But sometime during the night
Somewhere inside her
A miracle reservoir burst open
Vomiting a blood red sea

And she woke up
Frantic and vexed
Clinging for dear life
Onto the dead hands
Of a drowning innocence
Floundering without direction
And robbed of the will
To swim out to
The shores of yesterday

She went to bed a child
And woke up a woman
Imbued with a new voice
That spoke liltingly
Of pads and tampons
And rude labour pains

## VULTURE

Her love I swear
Is a cunning pickpocket
Nimble fingered
And extracting from
The wallet of my heart
Emotions preserved and
Saved
For that wintry day
When the fireplace
Of my existence
Shall boast only of cold ashes
Garnered from bonfires of old
When acquaintances would
the midnight oil burn
Warming me up
With blazing smiles
And fleece-lined lies

She comes to me today
As a time traveling vulture
One who intrudes into
The future of my affections
And feasts on the decaying flesh
Of dead relationships
That today thrive and bustle
With a counterfeit immortality

## FIRST KISS

He kissed like a bee
Deep into the core
Of my virgin aloofness
Where sweetness
Is a buried treasure
And lies hidden
In an unseemly corner
That shyness occupies
And awkwardness stands guard.

He stung like a bee
His tongue a heat seeking missile
That navigated itself
To the secret cauldron
In my mouth
Where saliva bubbled
In effervescent continuity
Distilling a warmth
That spread like oil
In a burning sea
Flowing throughout my body
And escalating temperatures
In areas that previously
Had housed cold decency

## PROSPECTOR

He said he was a prospector
Looking for virgin land
On which to drill and mine.

He said this as
He looked me over
With mineral detector eyes
That bored deep to my centre

He looked like no miner
That I knew
Clean shaven and dressed
To the sixes and nines,

He carried no toolbox
And I couldn't help but notice
That his long-fingered hands
Held nothing in them,

It was then that
I started wondering if
He meant to use them
For tools and equipment,

And I started feeling
Sorry for those hands
And prayed that in his prospecting
He would find a mine,

As soft as my breast.

# THOUGHTS ON THE NEW YEAR

....and so I stand alone
In that void
In between the years
Where time's hands
Are reduced to a mule
Laden with stillborn dreams
Headed into the morrow
Where yet another year waits
With gloved hands
To receive this gift
From a grateful past
Which now can in peace rest
Divested of this macabre baggage
That man puts his optimism on
Hoping that this season
The rotting dream-cadaver
Will somewhat revive
And like a mushroom
Suddenly shoot to growth
To add flavor to the soup
That the success-wishers
Feed on as they sharpen
Their faithful pencils anew
To inscribe fresh resolutions
On the scared face of fate

# OASIS

there are footprints in my mind
where your shadow trod
on its quest to outpace the body

they wink in the dark
like dancing fireflies
in the cold desert night

their passage
illuminating the spot
that yesterday you watered

to create an oasis
in the midst of my
barrenness

## SHADOWS

We are but shadows
Our existence is tied
To the benevolence
Of the sun
We live in abject terror
Of dark moonless nights
With yawning black mouths
Leading to tomb-like bellies
But sometimes in the day
When safety and assurance rule
Clouds blindfold the sun
Rendering us extinct

# REACHING OUT

Ascending the staircase
To your heart
I slipped and I fell
The thuds and groans
Resonating melodiously
with your disquiet

I wish for an affection
Gifted with wings
To soar above all hindrances
And sweetly deposit me
In the treasury of your heart
To explore its generosity

## THE SANDS OF TIME

The cock crows rudely
Startling peace and rest

And the sun pokes with
Ungentle finger

And the slumberer rouses
With regretful yawn

To face another arrogant day

*(I alone stand still*
*Unwelcoming the sands of time*
*Which bring siltation*
*To the fountain of youth*
*Till its waters are rendered impure*
*And none dare drink of it)*

## GOING HOME

On that anthill yonder
They buried my umbilical cord
And returned me to dust
The day I was born
Before I could comprehend
Termites had already feasted
on my dumbfounded being
And excreted the remnants
Into the latrine of oblivion
I roam this earth now
A bodied ghost inextricably drawn
To that dusty anthill
Where impatient termites
Await the main course
To the starter they tasted

## TEMPTRESS

It is hellish here
And dark as sin
Where the self sits
Inextricably bound
By throbbing veins
In the pumping station
Of her heart.
Where is the eastern star
That twinkled and winked
And lit my path
As I followed her voice
That sung of sweetness unsullied
Like the honey bird
Of the African badlands?

She comes now
Ever so frequently
Aboard the ship of
My dreams
Decked in captain's apparel
And steering my emotions
Towards isles so barren
That no joy can sprout.

# GOOD MORNING TENANT

Wish me not
A good morning
When your rasping voice
Borrows its character
From my wife's knee-shuffle
As she scrubs to unnecessary lustre
The tired corridors of your house
Under the gaoler-gaze of your wife
And your Peeping Tom forays
That seek perverted delight
In shooting arrows of debauchery
In my wife's direction
As she goes about her industry
Serving the sentence that society
Imposed on the untitle-deeded
In this nation of sons of the soil.

## SUNRISE

Last night
I shared my bed
With the sun
I covered it all
In warm covers
Such that its light
It could not shed
On anyone but me

I remember its hot body
Sneaking into my blankets
Like Ruth to Boaz did
On that definitive day
When brazenness replaced modesty
And the hunter became
The hunted
And a generation was
Planted

I remember its hot breath
Touching my every part
With fiery passion and intent
Like the firestorm
That razed Sodom and Gomorrah
Putting to bed once for all
Lewdness and unwholesome libidos

This morning I woke up
To the embrace of a cold dawn
Whose caresses wrote
A script devoid of excitement
On the tremulous scroll
Of my tingling body
And rising from a distance

Its face turned a blushing gold
I saw the sun of my night
Boldly fornicate with
Granite hearted mountains,
Siring and at once conceiving
A radiant infant-morn

# SHOOTING STAR

I saw a shooting star fall
With its finger on the trigger
Blazing till the death
It looked like it was
Fleeing heaven
To seek refuge in
The heathen embrace
Of a stoic earth
Whose hunchbacked form
Mirrored the grotesque appetites
Of demons abiding
In fiery fury
In its boiling gut

# DICTION

Words
When birthed by
The forced union
Between violent vowels
And raped consonants
Exhibit a temper unmanageable
They kick
Fine tuned phrases
Into senseless gibberish
Leaving them sore
And paralyzed
And strung into weeping
Limping sentences
That will at once
Dazzle and befuddle...
Till a connoisseur with
Archimedean ecstasy
Emerges naked from
A dip in encyclopedic waters
Grasping a choked verse
Which gasps astounded
Like a beached mermaid.
Stunned and undeafeaned
To its captor's shout of
"Eureka!!"

# EMPTY TALK

I have had conversations
With empty beer bottles
I have listened quietly
To tear wrenching tales
From these hitherto carriers
Of a potency distilled to pose
As wit and wisdom

They told me
Father drank his all
One queer day
When the sun rose
From the west
Sending birds into
Confused slumber,

And with much the same aplomb
Without shame or remorse
The contents of the bottles
slew father

# FORLORN

Sometimes loneliness
Has enticing appeal
It courts you with
Dusty visage
Punctuated by
A gap-toothed smile
Triggered by none
Other activity
But the sight of you
Seated upon your dreams
In this forlorn corner
Of God's creation
Where barrenness is
The way of life
Even in the face of
Fertile reflections
Garnered from a world-weary soul
Whose feet have chosen
Their own itinerary
And led one to perch
On the seat of a silence
Loaded with whisperings
Of ancient and endless gods
Whose remains remain buried
Under the scorching earth
But whose spirit
Will eternally roam in reign
In this land of grotesque grandeur

## SUSPICION

What if the cows
Do not come home
What if they are
Also missing from the pasture?
Will that peaceable crocodile
Who has lived all his life
In still waters
Where the herd drank
And sated mammoth thirsts
Without losing any of their number:
Will such crocodile
Who has suppressed
Natural inclinations
To feed on mud like catfish
Will he be looked at
With same regard and tolerance,
When the cows do not come home
And there's silence
In the kraals?

# NOMADS

Today I shall pass by
That intersection once more
Where cars ferrying travellers
Of fate and chance converge
Some driving into unknown lands
To seek the destiny of their imaginations
And others following like accidental disciples
in fervent pursuit
Fleeing their own demons

I shall look away again today
When the one-legged beggar
Propped up on expensive crutches
Extends a well-fed arm
Seeking alms
Under the unaffected witness
Of glass-eyed traffic lights
That glare and stare
And wink authoritatively
With reddened eyes
And for a transient moment
Coalesce nomadic strangers
To outstare each other
with rude wonderment
As they pause from
treading tedious roads
that lead to nowhere

## DAYS THAT MATTER

The days that matter
Are not these
That sit stagnant
On the calendar
Staring endlessly at eternity
Whilst the throat of time
Has vomited them
Into the pit toilet
Where clean futures
Frequent to spew
Diarrheal discharges
Into the path of hope
Days that matter
Are yet to be born
These I see in my dreams
Days not strung together
In seconds and minutes
On the strings of patience
Like the waist beads
Of a pagan temptress
Enticing and mysterious
And open to exploration
By any who would
Muster courage
To stare and wink

## WET DREAMS

He stood in the rains
As wet dreams
Fell with shameless abandon
From the heavens
He stood without umbrella
Soaking to the bone
But somewhere at his centre
A fire burnt persistently
And refused to be doused
He felt a heat colonise him
And his body responded
Tinglingly with pleasure-pain
He wanted to scream
He wanted to dance
He wanted to laugh,
But still he remained rooted
Married to the muddy reality
And the slippery hope
That impossible it was
To successfully navigate
And so he lingered there
Lifting his face to the skies
Seeking to glimpse the face of She
Who always came faithfully
As drizzle of healing rain
During times of drought
When seeded affection
Lay burning and dying
In girls' rocky hearts

## SELF POTRAIT

im here
but you can't see me now
look
im cunningly disguised
like the smell within the fart
invisible but pervasive
occupying the space
that you flee
like the suppressed orgasmic scream
in the grab and toss confusion
of rapist-victim encounter

im here
a wordcrook
verbal ninja
slicing your thoughts
with deformed metaphor and form
twisting and turning in the intricacies
of your brain arena
a demented take-them-on and
make-them-see-dust-messi
reserving my best for moments
such as these
when with mouth agape
you salute with a saliva-drooled
WOW

# THOUGHTS

He dreamt his brain
Crept out of his head
Through his astonished eyes
Slithering unhurriedly
Like gooey excretion
Down his indifferent cheeks
It deposited itself
On his lap and there
Sat illuminating him
With frantic thoughts
Whose mesmerizing fingers
Stitched haphazardly
Multi-coloured patches
To cover glaring holes
On his thinking cap
Using his emotions
As thread and his
Ambition as needle

He longed to swat at it
As one would, a fly, kill
And destroy all the smugness
Housed in its grey cells
Where scales
Calibrated to measure
His worth against
Peers, kith & kin
Enjoy pride of place

So he glared at it
With stabbing looks
That perforated its exterior
And entered its core
And there surprised he
Truth and myth

Sitting entwined in
Easy copulation
Striving to conceive
A child of nameless pedigree
One that neither hungers
Breathes nor dies

# CALENDAR

Here, days abide
Imprisoned in paper cells
And locked in place
By padlocks of ink
I look at them
And wonder
At their stoic loyalty
In staying at their
Allotted station without
Deviation day by day.

They got tales to tell
Some sad some tall
Some about the day
Mother missed her period
And she came and
Stared and stared
At them
As if willing them
To go back to those times
When the plumber
Was not such a temptation
And father was not such a brute

They tell too tales
Of the day
When in silence
Sister came high
On illicit substances,
Circled the day's date
And began to mutter that
As long as she had time
On her hands
She could weave it

How ever she chose;
And in that instance
Her wrists, she
immediately slit

And as the life
Ebbed out of her,
She saw the dates
Looking at her
Without surprise
And with the smug look
Of one who is
On talking terms with fate
And knows beforehand
Each footprint imprinted
On the beach of tomorrow,

And knows too the
Exact moment in time
When a wave shall
From the seas emerge
And obliterate all
Traces of trails walked
Upon the sands of time.....

## TAKEN

Passion is a gun
Whose trigger is caressed by the emotions
The deafening blast and ardent spit
Is the disgusted expletive
Of the pure in man
But this unlikely love
Sired by cold steel and explosive gunpowder
And consummated in the blued gut of the bullet chamber
With death targeting the heart gleefully along eager barrel
Defies circumstance, form and time
In the demon infested gun powder fumes
Where weeping, teeth-gnashing butchered souls abound
Your huntress' instinct sweetly unhinges my resolve
And in the magical never-never land of your mouth
I discover to the completion of my doom
That elixir and the forbidden fruit
Are mutually exclusive treats

# WEDDING NIGHT

let love whisper a serenade
coaxed from the wind's
breathless symphony
and seduce the rainbow
with the dainty giggles
of rose tickled faeries
sweetly disrobing it
of its virginal robes
of mating colors
to adorn the bride's
bashful innocence
for the honeymoon altar

# EPITAPH

His fate was writ in water
Penned by the wind
In its gentler moments
Abhorring the salty destination
That awaited him
In the seas of commonality
He departed
Silently with vapour stealth
Leaving his legacy hanging angrily
Like stormy clouds
Threatening to burst torrentially
And create oases of hope
In the deserts of our mourning

## LEAVING HOME

This road today
I know we walked it
Before in times
When it pointed to
Horizons unexplored
Where rainbows
Mated with sunsets
To bring to life
A world so dreamy
And tantalizing
A world so enticing
That we forgot
The pain of trekking
And the sweet call
Of mother's voice
As she hummed that
Ageless hymn
Whilst coaxing the
Tired soils that
Now refused to nourish
Even the hardiest seed
And yet day to day
To that field she
Her way she faithfully made
To fulfil the undying pact
That she had
With the rains made
To dig graves for
It's aborted droplets
Who fall to this earth
To gift life
A chance at life

# HEAVEN

Where now to turn to
And seek sanity
In a world where truth
Is found hidden
In the undergarments
Of a harlot adorning
A nun's habit on
Snapchat and Instagram

The televangelist
Wears mini skirts
Preaching a gospel
Rinsed of divine aura
To a congregation that
Throngs in week after week
For a hopeful glimpse
Of the outline of the fruit
That Eve leafily covered

Father already has
His heaven figured
It smells of hops and barley
And stays imprisoned
In its metal can
Till he liberates it
Only to promptly consign it
To the gallows in his gut

But I love mother's
heaven the most
It smells of father
And earthen floors
And smoky fires
And damp mud
In the midst of drought

# FATHER'S DAY

He became a father
One drunken day
When the club spotlights
Connived with the cheeky mascara
And naughty lipstick
To carve a stunning beauty
Out of mother's poverty
Ravaged face

I tell you
He became a father
Somewhere in the back alleys
Of frontline brothels
Where orgasms are metered
And pleasure is counterfeit
And condoms pronounced reusable
Only to burst in protest
Showering seed into
Unprepared fields
But fertile all the same

He became a father
On a day when alcohol
Stole his memory
And rendered him comatose
And so to his shirtless
Wandering he retired
To wake up the morrow
Without recollection of
The arable land he had ploughed
And the seed he had planted

Today mother frequents
Still the same bar

And stares at the door
For times without end
Willing the wind to blow
Him in from wherever
He had hailed from,
If only to let him know
That he now qualifies
To receive Father's Day wishes
In earnest and in truth

## POT SHOT

He went out
Hunting for anything
On which to build
His satedness atop
He left behind
Empty pots and
Unlit kitchen fires
And took with
Him for companionship
The impatient rumbling
Of a vacuous stomach

He saw her
Standing innocently
In her neighbourhood
Rooted where she
Had every right to be
That thicket where
Her ancestors had
Roamed free and proud
With the only enemies
Known to them
Being four legged
And fierce toothed

She saw in him
A peaceable curiosity
While his eye registered
A succulent possibility
On his quest for
gastric gratification

He shot without thinking
And as his missile

Found her bewildered heart,
She had him exclaim
In a manner eerily orgasmic

And the last thing she saw
Was him salivating profusely
As if the fires
In his famished mind
Had already been ignited
By the passage of her spirit
Enroute to other realms
Where the essence of her being
Was not a component
For culinary consideration

## NOMADS

Today I shall pass by
That intersection once more
Where cars ferrying travelers of fate and chance converge
Some driving into unknown lands
To seek the destiny of their imaginations
And others following like accidental disciples
in fervent pursuit
Fleeing their own demons
I shall look away again today
When the one-legged beggar
Propped up on expensive crutches
Extends a well-fed arm
Seeking alms
Under the unaffected witness
Of glass-eyed traffic lights
That glare and stare
And wink authoritatively
With reddened eyes
And for a transient moment
Coalesce nomadic strangers
To outstare each other with rude wonderment
As they pause from treading tedious roads
that lead to nowhere

# GLOBAL WARMING

Who smoked a joint
And blew the smoke
Into the earth's sober face?
Now it's wobbling drunkenly
On the axis of its seasons
And can't tell winter from summer.
It is sobbing violently
In great stormy gales
And coughing out
Monsoons and tsunamis
Every other day.
Who smoked the joint
And blew it out
From factory sized nostrils
Now the stoned earth
Is spinning in reverse
Lifting up its skirts
To fart now and then
At innocent skies
Who disgusted roll away
Their protective blanket
To expose the bare bottomed planet
For the heavy-handed attentions
Of the toxic-tempered sun
To spank at will
Without any restraint

## LOVE TREK

I walked the lonesome mile
From your brain to your heart
I carried nothing but words
Robbed from dead man's books
Words that had battled with time
And came out deformed and deranged
But words that manufactured still
Silky banter and fragrant garb
To dress and soothe the wounds
Festering in the chambers of your heart

# SUSPICION

What if the cows
Do not come home
What if they are also
Missing from the pasture?

Will the peaceable crocodile
Who has lived all his life
In still waters
Where the herd drank
And sated mammoth thirsts
Without losing any of their number:

Will such crocodile
Who has suppressed
Natural inclinations
To feed on mud like catfish
Will he be looked at
With same regard and tolerance,

When the cows do not come home
And there's silence
In the kraals?

# THE COLORS OF VALENTINE

Red
The color of blood
Seen only when
Injury calls and pain
Visits

Black

The color of mourning
Worn only when
Death visits and grief
Calls

But

In love still I believe
And my heart to you
Without doubt I give

Though

The past is black clad
And my soul still weeps
Red endless tears

## WEEPING HEARTS

Your memory
A soiled handkerchief
Lies folded in the
Side pockets of the tuxedo
The undertaker adorned
To be taken out as needed
To help broadcast a
Counterfeit grief to
The gallery of weeping hearts
Angel tears
Disguised as stars
Cleave into the tapestry
Of the sky's blanket
Wrapped around the casket
Containing the remains
Of kamikaze adoration

## HEAVEN BOUND?

And the soul hereby stands
Mired in the inter stellar
Quagmire of black holes
Rogue meteorites
And numbing darkness
This the route to heaven
It must navigate
Aboard spaceships
Of prayers launched off
When it was still docked
In the flimsy abode
It naively called home

## MARAH

I met her
In the streets
Of her laughter
Walking alone and
Trailed by shadows
Of yesteryear mirth
Carrying a bag with
Dainty giggles and
Bellowing guffaws
Battling to harvest
Flawless smiles from
My lonely heart

## MPENDWA

You waft around me
Like coloured scented mist.
I see but can't possess you
As you dance around me
With maddening allure
Intoxicating me with that heady fragrance
Reminiscent of the forbidden fruit
Which beguiled Eve with promises
Of mysterious and unheard-of flavour

But when you are not there
You mutate and become tear smoke
Bringing tears to my eyes
Your absence strangling my heart
So in the season of your desertion
I choke on my loneliness
Waiting for the breeze of your re-entry
Into the galaxy of my solitude
To gift me relief

# CONTEMPLATION

I sat on the edge of sanity
Perched precariously
On doubt's seat
Holding on for dear life
To the petticoats of reason
Covering the immodesty
Of habit and custom
Who sat open-legged
And shameless
On that famed crossroad
Where wit battles emotion
To entice the wayfaring being
To walk trails that
Have no name
And whose coordinates
Are found engraved
On sanatorium walls
In cryptic script
That only the condemned
Can decipher...

## MEMORIES OF MOTHER

I walk these endless trails
In brooding thankless forests
Seeking to find the spot
That they buried the umbilical cord
That bound me to mother
I want to exhume it
And bathe it with my tears
So gently and so lovingly
In the manner mother did
When I soiled myself
And she wiped me clean
With a smile on her lips
And a song in her soul
I want to pray over it
Such that it comes to life
With vigor and new purpose
In much the same way
That mother interceded
And invoked divinity
When my hopes lay disemboweled
And flies of despair
Gorged on the remains
I walk these nameless trails
Humming lullabies that
She used to croon
And I would hitch myself
On the wings of her lilting voice
To be transported to dreamy slumber-land
Peopled by images of
Her restful face

## MEMORIES OF MOTHER II

There is the rocking chair
On which she sat
It abides right there
Under the changeable shade
Of the barren mango tree
Waiting for her
To come and perch
On its creaky lap
And begin their
Undulating ride,

Up and down
Down and up

I wasn't around
To witness her fall
But I found her down
Fallen from her chair
Which now continued
It's journey companion-less,

Down and up
Up and down

I stared at her fallen
And willed her to rise
Like her wooden companion
To spring from her fall
For times without count,

Down and up
Up and down

But alas for mother
Her body remained

Down and down
But her spirit
Like a bullet
Shrieked through
unknown realms
Going doggedly
Up and up....

## WILL THE BEES RETURN

Will the bees return
Once they have disrobed
Innocent flowers of
Their dainty attire
And drunk to the full
Their fill of nectar
From under the skirts
Of innocent flowers?
What's left for the flowers
Except to lie wilted
And dry mouthed
In green meadows
Undefeaned to the
Incessant buzz of
Worker bees as they
Pass by without a glance
Searching without end
For their unspoilt kith
To swindle them
Of their sweetness
Leaving them gaping
And hollow-eyed

## BY MY SIDE, BE

We gathered early
One unremarkable morning
Putting our heads together
Like firewood in
Grandmother's hearth
Waiting for the
Spark of life
From an ember stolen
Sometimes from the bonfire
That mourners congregate around
As they maintain vigil
To keep the newly
Disembodied soul, company.

Will you still,
By my side, be
When blazing words
Come flying from
Lips empowered by
Our lack of restraint
Head towards our
Straw bed and pillow
In some knowing lodge
Where forbidden love
Is afforded metered tolerance

# SUITOR

He sought her heart
Aboard chariots of fervour
With none to bear witness
Save for the snoring night
And the mouthless moon

He entered through
The pools in her eyes
And swam through
Oceans of bloodied tears
To land triumphant
On the shores
Of her secluded heart

He walked barefoot
On the sands
Of her affection
Leaving deep footprints
That even gales of scorn
Would blow in vain
To eradicate

And she saw him
Approach determinedly
As she pulled shut
The curtain of her consent
Leaving him to roam
The perimeters of her
Magnetic desirability
In confused hope

## TO LIE IN STATE

Recycled pity
Struggles to put on
A new sorrowful mask
With counterfeit tears
Empty voices howl
At the skies
Frightening the stars
And some crash to the earth
Like Lucifer after Michael's
Robust punch
Bussed in presidents
Pick their noses and curse
At the bitter obstacles
In Candy Crush
And Talking Tom's
Uncultured farts
And she lies in state
With just as much interest
In commoners' affairs
As she had whilst
Welded to the throne

## KUMAVAMBO

In the beginning
Before the earth was
Where was it?
Was the earth
Imprisoned in heaven's
Mighty expanse
And in the beginning
The earth was released
Dusty and scarred
And became the earth?
If that then be so
Is heaven akin to earth
And earth a heaven's clone?
How interesting could
Life then become
If the earth were heaven
And heaven were earth
We would look down
To witness the stars
And climb down trees
To harvest their fruits
This then your beginning
Which has no beginning
Cannot have an end
We abide in wonder
Traversing our existence
Aboard chariots of time
Whose genesis we know not
But whose ending
We seem to fathom
In shovels of dirt
Thrown into finite graves
Foolishly seeking to inhibit
Infinite beings

# TALK IS CHEAP?

They told him
That talk is cheap
And so he headed out
To the nearest market
Where it rumoured was
That words persuasive
And phrases witty
Were available for
The taking by those
With few grey cells
In the torn pockets
Of their intellect.

So he bartered his arms
For a bushel of tired idioms
And sold off a bit of leg
For a dictionary of dead phrases
Garnered from dead languages
That the living dead
Thought fashionable to utter
Sometimes in courts of law
Where unfashionably-clad judges
Pronounced dire sentences
That reeked of death

He made his way home
Now empowered
His tale to tell
But found everyone
With ears plugged
And tongues cut off
Talking each to the other
In sign language

## NESTLINGS

He dreamt of vultures
And of thoughts
That were nestlings
With wings that
Still feared to unfurl
And so remained trapped
In prickly nests
On some imposing tree
In the jungle of his mind.

He dreamt of stormy winds
And woodsmen bearing
Sharp toothed axes
And dreamt too
Of empty hearths
With mouths agape
Waiting to be fed,
Same as nestlings....

## POTATO TALE

I'm a potato
Not colourful
Not glamorous
Just me
A potato...
Sometimes
I'm found
In the company
Of tomatoes
Bright red
Smooth skinned
Creatures of
High appeal and demand
I'm a potato
I don't rate
My chances highly
But always
The ladies
Who frequent the market
Jostle to have me first
Right under
The envious gaze
Of the juicy tomato
Whom same as I
Fails to comprehend
Why a simple jacketed
Dry being with
Neither sweet scent
Nor savory juice
Always tops
The shopping list
Of connoisseurs whose
Taste buds crave satisfaction

# AM I MAD?

There are voices in the wind
Gentle soothing voices
That whisper ceaselessly to me
Urging me to leap off
The cliffs of my security
Down into the dark void
Where nightmares and fears are conjured
And where reality takes a mutant form
To become the bogey man
That mother warned me about
In bedtime tales that robbed me
Of every hope of restful slumber
And substituted my dreams
With the promise of nightmares
There is commotion in my mind
And raucous debate
As the accusers
The martyrs
The lynch mob
All bang furiously at the walls of my reason
Engaging me in constant bickering
Till the death of night

# DESERTION

When birds
Have flown the nest
To no more return
They carry their song
With them leaving behind
A disquieting quiet
They swallow
Their footprints
And obliterate traces
Of their journey
With the patient nest
They sweep away all
Even their shadows
And the scent that
Once spelt home
Leaving an odorless
And sterile abode
That even dust
Fears to settle on

# CENSUS

She has been
Sitting there for
A while now
Empty eyes
Staring at the
Silent heavens
Counting stars
Her concentration
Is utmost
She is dead to all
But her onerous task,
Dead even to
The homing flies
Now nestled at
The corners of
Her mouth
Like living lipstick
Dead even to
The sandy dust
Now hardened around
Her unblinking eyes
Like caked excreta
That tears can't flush
I have watched
For more than a while
Seeing her lips
Frame numbers
Alien to my comprehension,

Psychollions
Crazillions
Madillions
Insanillions.

I would gladly

Have helped her
In her census
But only it is noon
And there are no
Stars visible
In the skies

## LIFE

We all are cigars
Rolled by the
Hands of chance
To co-exist and be
Packed without choice
In a creased packet
That we call home
Our world subsists
Eternally imprisoned
In the torn pockets
Of a tired karma
Whose unerring
Hand without ado
Fishes one from
Our midst at whim
Promptly lighting it
On a hellbound fiend's
Foul fiery footprints
Drawing hard on
The soul of the
Condemned cigar,
And blowing the smoke
Right into the face of God

# THOUGHTS II

There are grey areas
In grey matter
And the confounded brain
Scratches it's head
Seeking to find healing.
From the ravages
That battling thoughts
Inflicted seeking clarity
Aborted computations
Howl in throbbing anguish
Seeing no answers
To the barrage
Of questions and riddles
And quizzes and teasers
That the being pumps
Into the perpetual
Think-tank where
Reason lies dissected
Its innards exposed
To the gluttony of
Self-consuming doubts

## LULLABY

These songs
That you sing
Whose words
Dance on my soul
Making my head
Dislodge and spin,
And my eyelids
To trip and fall,
These songs
I don't want
To hear no more.

Sing me no lullabies
No more for me
The soothing melodies
For this black sleep
That now beckons
Has neither beginning
Nor ending
It wears eternity's cloak
And has a grip unrelenting
And on its bosom
I shall faithfully lie
Oblivious to all but
This forced romance
Which will beget
Neither redemption
Nor condemnation
But only a dark black
Sameness

## FORTUNE SEEKERS

And so we stopped moving
And down we sat
In the middle of the road
We had come from afar
Riding the rusty chariots
Of unhygienic dreams
Seeking to appease this hunger
That sought to ransack
And rob every horizon
Of its rainbow and swindle it
Of its pot of gold
And out in the distance
At the point where
Lunacy and ambition merge
A shy sun arose
Wedded to a misty haze
Conjuring a rainbow
Gigantic and alluring
Which to us winked
With bewitching promise
And so promptly we stood
On blistered feet
Barely rested
To pick up the chase
Once more
Clothed in beggar rags
And rich optimism

## VOICE OF SILENCE

Silence

Which mouth agape
Spittled lips
Industrious tongue
Yet without voice

Silence

Pregnant with untold tales
Raped by world weary souls
Howling, screaming
Yet with confused pleasure

Silence

Loaded with whisperings
From ancient gods of garb
Constipated and farting
Deafeningly in the face of reason

## THE DAY WHEN PIGS FLEW

The day when pigs flew
Was as empty as any other
The sky for all its elegance
Was nude and starless
And sat scratching its privates
In full glare of a peeping tom-sun
It was the day when
The dollar wrestled THE DOLLAR
And was pronounced victor
By a blind-as-bat judge
Who mistook cries of horror
For raucous applause
It was that January day
When father having imbibed
Tichaona's school money
During unbridled December festivities
Posted to the school head
November herald headlines
Proclaiming with executive aplomb
"Free Education for All"
It was the day when
Social media seers
Chanting chillingly from
Facebook and WhatsApp shrines
Prophesied of dead African bodies
Piled up and rotting
In covid-fouled streets

# DARK WORLD

It is a dark world
When the stars
Have to seek
The night's permission
For them to shine

When black-hearted witches
Count the serene moon
Amongst the paramount
Of their paramours
It indeed is darkblack

The voices of the night
Will the land rape
Scaring the deflowered Zambezi
Into the belly of Nyami Nyami
Whilst Kariba opens her mouth,
Seeking to slack
Ancient thirsts and appetites
Only to be fed
Prayers and petitions
In a language strange,
By counterfeit priests
Who seek to use fingers
To milk interventions
From barren rosaries
Sold for a song
At every street corner
And in shebeens and brothels
And backyard surgeries
Where light lies aborted
Fly-feasted and rotten

# DEATH OF A STATUE

The statue was dying
With none to hold its hand
It had stood there
Proud and imperious
Without breaking sweat
In the heat of the day
Nor shivering
In the arms
Of a spitting cold

The statue was dying
Tattooed by the cracks
That pretended to be wrinkles
But were sly fissures
inviting death to hammer in
The chisel that chipped off
Immortality and eternity,

The statue was dying
And none took notice
Save for a passing crow
That dumped its stool
On the statue's face
And crowed away in
Bewildering glee

## UPON SEEING RHODES' CARRIAGE AT A MUSEUM
## IN BULAWAYO

I saw the carriage
That carried Rhodes
And I wondered
How it managed to contain
The baggage in his mind
Cape to Cairo railroad dreams
And Kimberley diamonds
And Mashonaland gold

I looked into the interior
So opulent but eerie
A true velvet-lined coffin
In bleeding crimson
Like Dracula's coat
An interior fit to match
A vampire appetite

I peeped and I wondered
Which seat the devil took
When they together held counsel
To desecrate Dzimbahwe
And pilfer the guardian birds
To leave a whole people
Bereft of watchers
And so exposed to rude religions

I wondered what the devil saw
In that ruddy face and serpent eyes
Was he aghast at the absence
Of conscience and guilt?
Or with a vile chuckle,
It dawned on him
That finally he had
His match met

And so had to girdle up
Or surrender his throne
To this Englishman
Boasting blue eyes
And a black heart

# AT THE CROSSROADS

at the crossroads
we shall meet
you coming your way
and I mine
pausing to appraise one another
in that curious self-conscious manner
that strangers possess

at the crossroads
we shall linger
you contemplating your next turning
and I mine
wondering idly at the other's actions
in that curious self-conscious manner
that strangers possess

at the crossroads
we shall part
you going your own way
and I mine
turning our backs on each other
and pursuing two different rainbows
for the same pot of gold

## HERE I WILL ABIDE

I don't know where death resides
Nor where it is right now
I don't know what games
It is playing
Nor the schemes it is planning
But I know for certain
From the beating of my heart
And the warmth of her body
That death is not yet here
So here I will abide
And not move an inch
Even though enigmatic roads
Wink and beckon
Pointing to silhouettes of
titillating destinations
From here I won't depart
I will forever stay
Secure in the padlock
Of your embrace
Of which death knows not
The key to open up
And wrest me away

# DEATH OF TIME

He took me into a room
Where the skeletons of time
Lay unburied and piled up
Forgotten without a monument
Erected for their commemoration
These are the seconds
That breezed round the
Clocked face of eternity
He whispered huskily
They thought that
By fleeing the past
They would find the future
He chuckled sagely
But here they lie dead
Spewed from the mouth
Of a fate that chewed the present
Tasted endless tomorrows
And vomited the past

## WOOER

He spoke in straight lines
His words leaving
The nest of his heart
And heading straight for mine
As the crow flies

He smiled crookedly
But still straight mirth
Shot from the bow
Of his bubbling eyes
And found my heart unerringly
Like Shaka's assegai

# DEATH OF A STATUE II

..and so there he lay
In a wooden box
Putting on a wooden smile
Seeming to find death such a joke
Just as life had once been
His eyes remained open and dry
Staring back disinterestedly
At those who professed
To have come to pay
Their last respects
Though he remembered not the moment
When he had received
Their first respect
He felt them tiptoe past
As if a heavy tread
Would him, from
This darkblack sleep, awaken
And he wondered
How such could be
An unwelcome occurrence
When they broadcast such naked grief
Though they be decked
In fashionable attire
that competes
And maybe wins
Against the sombre suit
That he wore
To present himself
Before divine council
As if for an interview

## DONKEY TRAIL

Today I want to try
And be a donkey's companion
Not shunning dusty trails
But slowly plodding on
Knowing that it pays not
To chase horizons
When the past
Is a burden that refuses
To be shed off as
One chases the future
I shan't use the whip
I want to follow
And be led to those places
That donkeys go to
If there is none to whip them
And their eyes are unblinkered
Maybe there I will find
Green pastures that
I can without a bank card access
And find too, I may,
Peace and solace
Far different from the cacophony
Of farting exhausts
Shrilling police sirens
And belching factory chimneys

# WHY LOVE IS PAIN

1
bitches
in
heat
tails held up
dripping love nectar
enslaving males

2
scarred
heart
weeping
disfigured beyond
attractiveness
repulsing attention

3
love
spurned
soul
finding no solace
in fledgling affection's
maiden flight
doomed to
end in crushed dreams
and broken hopes

4
past wounds
rose-disguised
with scented allure
boast of
a bite cruel
with thorny venom
poisoning the soul

and changing love's dove
into a hate breathing dragon

# THE FINAL CONDEMNATION

discarded, shredded and alone
left to rot unattended
in the valley of wet bones
and weeping flesh
till you come swooping down
with greedy heart and cruel beak
sinking your talons into the residue
of emotions once alive but plundered
picking me clean of any seed
of redemption and resurrection
saving me from the vagaries of
slow worm worn decay
For the hellish fumes in
the incinerator of your gut
and the reflection of the stoked fires
in your unblinking eyes

# DEADWOOD

We met on the hearth of chance
Putting dry heads together
Waiting for the hand
Of he who has the matchstick
To ignite us.

We met having come
From different paths
Having been felled
By different axes
But still we carried
The same scars
And knew the same pain

Fate pushed us here
To coalesce as thus:
Dry and forsaken
Reduced to flammable fuel
Destined to die
Offering light and warmth
To a dark meaningless world

## DEFLOWERED

The night came
And found us seated
Holding hands
Conversing in silence
Lying on the bed
Of our unmade dreams
Just us two.
When morning came
He had a grin and a glow
And she sat by his side
With thread and needle
Valiantly trying to repair
Dreams of perfect weddings
And proud hymens
On honeymoon nights

## MUSIC, LOVE & YOU

Loving you is like
Dancing on a razor's edge
With feet unshod
Balancing like a trapeze artist
On the thin line
Demarcating loyalty and stupidity
Enslaved to pain and peril
But still waltzing away
Goaded on by the whipping
Of guitar string and piano wire
And the cruel thumping
Of the bass drum and congas
While the penny whistle
Ululates its glee

## MAZES

There are mazes in the mind
Past which every thought
Must of fate navigate
To become a brain wave
In the seas of consciousness
Where hope and regrets cavort
In uneasy alliance
And where ideas are birthed
To confound conformity

Where blind thoughts
Remain hopelessly lost
Forever doomed to wander
In the maze's fearsome valleys
Their cries for redemption
Packaged in silent pain
Like screaming locusts
Engulfed in the hot embrace
Of a rampant veldt fire.

## REPRESSION

There is no hope
When tomorrow's fear
Weds yesterday's anguish today

They shall sire a child
Bastard to the bone
And call him legitimacy

He shall rule with chains & whips
And his roar shall be like the roar
Of guns and rifles

He shall sneeze bullets and smoke
And belch fire and gunpowder
And fart death and call it life

He shall decree
And it shall be tremblingly done
On earth but not in heaven..

## VOTING DAY

I remember bumping into a ballot paper
So chaste and clean she was
With a virginal and pure whiteness
She winked with freshness and promise
As she wafted into my hands for a caress

I boldy led her to a private booth
Far removed from prying eyes
And there in the quietness of the moment
Consummated we our fledgling love

She gave me her fragile body
And I perfumed her with inky longing
Tattooing her body with the tale
Of my aspirations and dreams
Of my visions and inspirations

I left her pregnant with my seed
And soon she was in labour pains
She groaned and made moanful effort
And presented a child for my sight

A beastly brute
Stillborn but fearsome
Far divorced from the beauty of my longing

## THE RAINS

The rains visited last night
Tear drop rain
Trailing wet footprints
That scribbled their tale
Of hot and bitter excursions
Across denuded cheek-terrains
Headed nowhere but to their doom

Do not take the plough out mother
Yoke not the oxen father
For it is not every sky
That bears clouds fatherly enough
To ejaculate life bringing potency
To satisfy the dry throated need
Of immodest mother earth

## ESSENCE OF EXISTENCE

We are sculpted from dust
Same as deserts
Oases come too far
And too in between
Like tears on the face of the statue
Of the Unknown Soldier
Who concretized into immortality
Stands sentinel against death
On the hilly shrine where they consign
Latter comrades fallen in less glorious times
To lie in opulent sepulchres
While the affluent artfully dab their eyes
And the mistresses howl with pitiful anguish
As they mourn the hero who dodged poverty
And inventoried the scraps fallen from his tables
So that Lazarus could have none.

Our days are measured
In degrees of searing heat
And in gallons of sweated toil
And in straw baked brick piles
While dry mouthed and saliva robbed
We toil under the demanding sjamboks
Of godless overlords who strike
With Pharistic menace and accuracy

Arise eastern wind arise
Howl with mighty wrath
Howl from the spot where Moses stood
Alone with dust stricken face
Where with rod and God
He bullied the waters
And on desert like sand man trod in awe
To meet emancipation and the cured

bitter waters of the wilderness
To complete the rescue plan of God

# SUNSET

Death smells like roses
At evening time
When the sun dies
In the ancient arms
Of steadfast mountains
That have seen it all
But refuse to mourn anymore

Death smells like roses
Even when there are no noses
To pay homage to its scent
Which refuses to repose
When the whole world takes respite
But it lingers to occupy
The gardens of the mind
With unrelenting presence

Like a curse..

## LONESOME

The sun
Doesn't want
to rise today
I held its hand
It felt feverish to the touch

The sun
Has a temperature
It has taken bed rest
On carpeted skies
And is covered in fluffy clouds

The sun
Doesn't want to come out
And play with me
I wait solitary in my little corner
Shivering in lengthening shadows
Waiting for the day to pass
And for the sun to die
So I can befriend the moon...

# SCARS

this is the scar
that scorn dealt me
feel it if you will
doesn't bother me anymore
i salved it with disdain
and its almost healed now

let me show your another
where poverty bit deep
straight into my livelihood
tearing my prospects to shreds
i have dressed it with hope
and it hurts less now

this beauty on my forehead
i got punched by reality
left me blue and black
my innocence in tatters
but it hardened into experience
and serves me well now

but don't touch this one please
it's still tender and raw
where your unapologetic words
cut the vows that bound you to me
it weep-bleeds from the heart
and pains ceaselessly

## WEDDING NIGHT

let love whisper a serenade
coaxed from the wind's
breathless symphony

and seduce the rainbow
with the dainty giggles
of rose tickled faeries

sweetly disrobing it
of its virginal robes
of mating colors

to adorn the bride's
bashful innocence
for the honeymoon altar

# CONTEMPLATION

1

puffed up locomotive dreams
riding rails of fancy
derailed before destination

2

dreams
shattered by
wake-up alarms
lie naked 'n butchered-
sunlit...

3

..and still it remains
to abduct the consciousness
and flee with it
into the grey mists
of realities that once were
but now remain entombed
in haunted mausoleums
in an unkempt corner
of the mind's cemetery..

## NOTHING TO GIVE

i have nothing to give
not even hope
for it too is a lie
and walks with you
only as far as you
are willing to hold its hand

i really have nothing to give
not even this heart
for it too is a fraud
neglecting you without a thought
pumping first and truly
for the body that houses it

i have nothing more to give
'cause all of value was plundered
stripped naked mercilessly
and sucked of all its sweetness
leaving only this flaccid shell
that has nothing to give

## THE SEPERATION

i used to cry with the falling leaf
discarded from the tree
its destination, its doom

but now i cry with the branch
clumsy fingered
unwittingly letting go

in the leaf's free fall
part of the branch falls too
never to rise again

but though the two
be together doomed
the branch weeps the longest

sap-tainted tears
spiraling in a slow pilgrimage
down the indifferent trunk

and the wind
unseen and with unmusical glee
ululates its spite

and leafy hearts
all around  freeze
sensing death's seeking antennae

## TIRED TIRE

i will let my will lend wings
to this tarmac shunned tire
now befriended by the wind

i want to hear it whisper sagely
in swishing nostalgic tones
skyscraper tales of the concrete world

so removed from this peaceful glade
where we fly astride dreams

Author notes
Prompt [Tire Swing set up in a forest]

# BENEATH THE SURFACE

there is black in the rainbow
it shies from vision's probe
but reveals itself truly
to the soul that quests
to close its eye to glory
proffered in the common plate

it alone remains
when night sits the throne
and sheds off all colour
and skin-dips in inky oasis of hope
and models unabashed
in the theater of the astute

and so too
does discord embrace order
and enemies foes converge
to dress old wounds of conflict
gotten in myopic wars of old
when none dared undress the rainbow

to discover the unifying bond of black

# DOOMSDAYERS

today, I shan't put on your garment of creeds
tis lice-ridden and an ill fit
and causes itches on the private parts of my soul
tender sores which the heavy handed attentions
of your fire breathing gods can deign to cure not

the heaven of your words feeds from damnation's breast
and swarms perpetually with hope consuming  angels
who with tar-brush and black heart
deluge the rainbow of salvation
with the uninspiring hues of hellfire ash

let me take scouring brush and  carbolic soap
to scrub out where your Judas kiss blemished my cheek
in a kiss of life that was packaged in death
and the seeds of doom irrigated by your spittle
discovered fertile ground in my innocence

## You

who broke these fallow fields
with sure steady practiced strokes
planting with indiscriminate intent
despair hope tears laughter pain joy
and teaching too the fertility dance
intricately weaving your dainty all-knowing gliding
to move in tune with my awkward first steps

You

who craved for and captured this fledgling rainbow
still intact and unswindled of its pot of gold
plunging with miserly intent into the unspoilt wealth
hoarding pilfering squandering cursing worshipping abusing
swallowing whole and saving none for a rainy day
and of my conquest fashioning a colourful souvenir
to take pride of place in your victor's spoils

You

who watched keenly at fall of day
to espy the sun fall into unashamed fornication with the horizon
reducing passions into a kaleidoscope of fighting colours-burst
mortal enchanting imprisoning liberating exquisite common
waiting on hand to deliver the child so conceived
dark dank degenerate night that arrived with keen wolf howl
swaddled in starry bands of my irretrievable innocence

You

who dipped your much used chalice
into the sweet waters of my newly sprung fountain
salivating with insatiable vampire-appetite
drinking dipping gulping gorging claiming colonising
wallowing with distended belly atop my sweetly outraged tainted

purity
leaving me no ointment to soothe and heal newly discovered
wounds
at the point where with your invisible perfumed chains you bound
me to yourself

as you pulled me from boyhood into manhood.

## OUTCAST

sitting quietly in your brain
forlorn by the walls of your thought factory
sifting through the dumpsite of your imaginings
seeking to find a memento of the love
that once you bestowed upon me unstintingly

wandering frantically in the landscape of your heart
thirsty in the desert of your emotions
sifting through the sands of your affections
seeking to find a grain that holds me still in fond regard
and suck from it loves' soothing juices

to quench this devotion-spurned soul....

## THESE FILTHY HANDS

These filthy hands
all gnarled and calloused
have nursed tender saplings
to full limbed majesty
and courted the blushful rose
to show off its perfumed splendour
to a dazzled humanity

These filthy hands
that you look at and shudder
have quietened the lowing cow
and brought many a calf into the world
and coaxed the land
to bring out its plenty
to feed humanity

These filthy hands
that you would rather not put a ring on
have mended the sparrow's broken wing
to ensure the continuance of woodland serenades
that you write to your beloved about
in sonnets teary and sincere
hypnotising humanity.

## LAMENTATION

Mourn with me
cry with me

mourn for these silenced voices
whose story never shall be told
mourn for these plugged ears
no music ever shall they hear
mourn for these blinded eyes
now lit out-visionless

mourn for the murdered dead
whose eyes are still alive with eternal curse
mourn for the orphaned toddler
now weaned of innocence with a budding hatred
mourn for the widowed wife
now contemplating embraceless nights

horrors now in my mind sojourn
I will tell them with the tears I weep
I will hear them in the pounding of my heart
i will see them in the mystery of my dreams
I will live them till you set my people free...

# FORSAKEN

They told me that you had gone
closing the door quietly
and never looking back
fading slowly until you became
one with the horizon of your expectations.

you left me all the clutter
strewn about without care:
a bit of laughter here
a dash of tears there
aborted plans all over
budding dreams cleanly nipped
by the incisors of your departure

and echoing all around the emptiness
of the void that once was your place
I still hear the hesitation of your footsteps
Reverberating

## SLOW-MARCH

and still it remains..
to taunt the imagination
with the bittersweet after-taste
of the forbidden fruit....
to abduct the consciousness
and flee with it into the grey mists
of memories that once were
but must now remain entombed
in unyielding caskets
in an arid 'scape of the mind's cemetery

time piped the tune
and we danced the dance
stomping and high-kicking
during Youth's care free reign
we dared to dare and against winds of convention
blew our vainly puffed chests
only realising our folly
when the resultant saliva shrapnel
blinded us in explosive admonition

now the music
once loud and clear
begs a passage through the indifferent air
no rapture here but only a dull allure
as the tired feet discover their own rhythm
in a sober shuffle-waltz
to oblivion

## IMPRINTS OF PAIN

the imprints of your words
still linger in my mind
startlingly defined
heading grief-wards

the love that we planted
somewhat still stands
with boughs drooping downwards
as i water it with my tears

the promises that we pledged
in sugared midnight escapades
now turn bitter on my tongue
as i swallow my words

it hurts like yesterday
your decades old departure
cutting merciless at my heart
with the daggers of today.

# DREARY MORNING

I have had my share of dark days in my time
and I can't discount the joys of sunshine as well,

I have swung uninhibited on the swing of reflections
taunting the demons and celebrating with the angels

I have been robbed of that which makes a man a man
and came face to face with that which unmans a man

I have drank to dregs my share of the bitter cup:
without complaint- without bidding it pass

I have travelled the high road and lain in lowly taverns
slave to my whims- accountable to none

But when I think of the way my whole being
hungers for you without contentment

tears break down the barriers of my self-control
as i pen down these lines for you on this dreary morning

# PAST THE THRESHOLD

you smelled of death last night
as you danced away
all the expensive perfumes
the cigarette smoke
the unwashed body odours
could not quite put away
the smell of death
that followed you everywhere
like a curse

even the pulsating music
somehow managed to sound
forlorn and subdued
and for a moment I felt
the dancing throng freeze
as if to observe a minute's silence
at the passing away of your innocence

# NEGLECT

discarded plans
abandoned in the mind's ashtray
like cigarette ends

half-smoked dreams
drift lazily out of reach
teasing grim reality

the brain reeks of fraud
as truth's scalpel
exposes tentative thought

If you have enjoyed *Death of a statue*, consider these other fine books in the **New African Poets Series** from *Mwanaka Media and Publishing:*

*I Threw a Star in a Wine Glass* by Fethi Sassi
*Best New African Poets 2017 Anthology* by Tendai R Mwanaka and Daniel Da Purificacao
*Logbook Written by a Drifter* by Tendai Rinos Mwanaka
*Mad Bob Republic: Bloodlines, Bile and a Crying Child* by Tendai Rinos Mwanaka
*Zimbolicious Poetry Vol 1* by Tendai R Mwanaka and Edward Dzonze
*Zimbolicious Poetry Vol 2* by Tendai R Mwanaka and Edward Dzonze
*Zimbolicious: An Anthology of Zimbabwean Literature and Arts, Vol 3* by Tendai Mwanaka
*Under The Steel Yoke* by Jabulani Mzinyathi
*Fly in a Beehive* by Thato Tshukudu
*Bounding for Light* by Richard Mbuthia
*Sentiments* by Jackson Matimba
*Best New African Poets 2018 Anthology* by Tendai R Mwanaka and Nsah Mala
*Words That Matter* by Gerry Sikazwe
*The Ungendered* by Delia Watterson
*Ghetto Symphony* by Mandla Mavolwane
*Sky for a Foreign Bird* by Fethi Sassi
*A Portrait of Defiance* by Tendai Rinos Mwanaka
*Zimbolicious: An Anthology of Zimbabwean Literature and Arts, Vol 4* by Tendai Mwanaka and Jabulani Mzinyathi
*When Escape Becomes the only Lover* by Tendai R Mwanaka
ويَسهَرُ اللَّيلُ عَلَى شَفَتي...وَالغَمَام by Fethi Sassi
*A Letter to the President* by Mbizo Chirasha
*This is not a poem* by Richard Inya
*Pressed flowers* by John Eppel
*Righteous Indignation* by Jabulani Mzinyathi:
*Blooming Cactus* by Mikateko Mbambo
*Rhythm of Life* by Olivia Ngozi Osouha

*Travellers Gather Dust and Lust* by Gabriel Awuah Mainoo
*Chitungwiza Mushamukuru: An Anthology from Zimbabwe's Biggest Ghetto Town* by Tendai Rinos Mwanaka
*Zimbolicious: An Anthology of Zimbabwean Literature and Arts, Vol 5* by Tendai Mwanaka
*Because Sadness is Beautiful?* by Tanaka Chidora
*Of Fresh Bloom and Smoke* by Abigail George
*Shades of Black* by Edward Dzonze
*Best New African Poets 2020 Anthology* by Tendai Rinos Mwanaka, Lorna Telma Zita and Balddine Moussa
*This Body is an Empty Vessel* by Beaton Galafa
*Between Places* by Tendai Rinos Mwanaka
*Best New African Poets 2021 Anthology* by Tendai Rinos Mwanaka, Lorna Telma Zita and Balddine Moussa
*Zimbolicious: An Anthology of Zimbabwean Literature and Arts, Vol 6* by Tendai Mwanaka and Chenjerai Mhondera
*A Matter of Inclusion* by Chad Norman
*Keeping the Sun Secret* by Mariel Awendit
سِجِلٌّ مَكْتُوبٌ لِثَائِهِ by Tendai Rinos Mwanaka
*Ghetto Blues* by Tendai Rinos Mwanaka
*Zimbolicious: An Anthology of Zimbabwean Literature and Arts, Vol 7* by Tendai Rinos Mwanaka and Tanaka Chidora
*Best New African Poets 2022 Anthology* by Tendai Rinos Mwanaka and Helder Simbad
*Dark Lines of History* by Sithembele Isaac Xhegwana


**Soon to be released**

*a sky is falling* by Nica Cornell
*The politics of Life* by Mandhla Mavolwane
*Along the way* by Jabulani Mzinathi
*Strides of Hope* by Tawanda Chigavazira


https://facebook.com/MwanakaMediaAndPublishing/

Printed in the United States
by Baker & Taylor Publisher Services